Piano Sketches

Vitalij Neugasimov

Book 2

14 intermediate pieces for solo piano

MUSIC DEPARTMENT

OXFORD
UNIVERSITY PRESS

UNIVERSITY PRESS

Great Clarendon Street, Oxford OX2 6DP,
United Kingdom

Oxford University Press is a department of the University of Oxford.
It furthers the University's objective of excellence in research, scholarship,
and education by publishing worldwide. Oxford is a registered trade mark of
Oxford University Press in the UK and in certain other countries

Database right Oxford University Press (maker)

First published 2016

Impression: 5

ISBN 978–0–19–341328–3

Music and text origination by Katie Johnston

Printed in Great Britain on acid-free paper by
Caligraving Ltd, Thetford, Norfolk.

Pieces from this collection originally published as part of
Pianoheads Collection 1 and *2* (2009 and 2010)

Contents

Composer's Note

Welcome to this short series of piano miniatures covering a broad spectrum of musical styles and gestures. Accessible yet engaging, the pieces should appeal melodically and harmonically to developing pianists, and provide opportunities for exploring musical textures and narrative while addressing technical points. They are written for player and listener alike, and hopefully inspire a sense of creativity and wonder at the palette of sound that is available to us.

This collection is dedicated to the memory of my beloved father, Vasilij Neugasimov. The pieces were inspired by my sister Liudmila Neugasimova, an outstanding piano teacher with over 20 years' experience; her encouragement and contribution were immense. I should like to thank, also, Martynas Vilkelis, who helped me to achieve my goal.

Country Fiddler

Vitalij Neugasimov

Annoying Fly

Vitalij Neugasimov

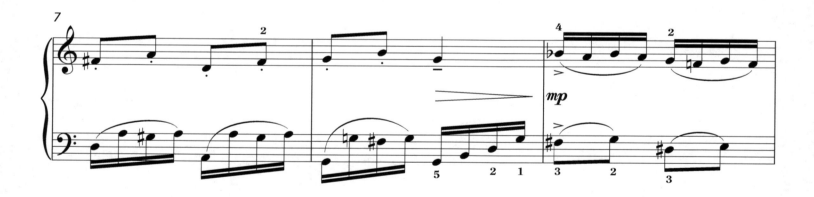

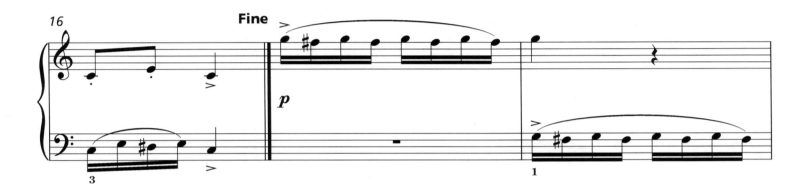

Funny Little Stride

Vitalij Neugasimov

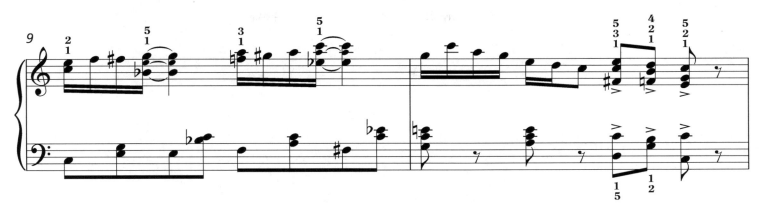

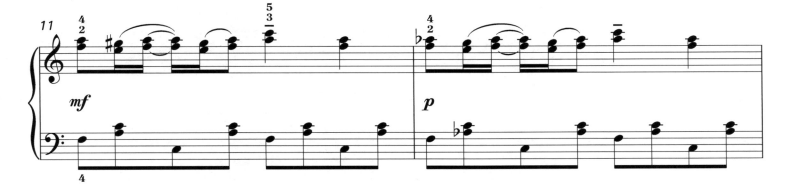

Baby Star

Vitalij Neugasimov

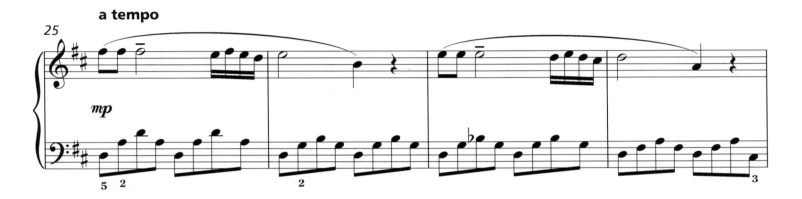

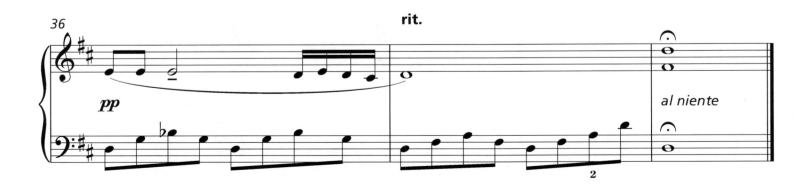

Blue Rondino

Vitalij Neugasimov

Allegro ♩ = 80

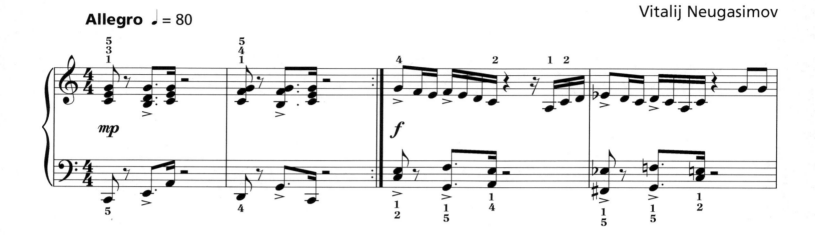

Sweet Memories

Vitalij Neugasimov

D.C. al Coda

CODA

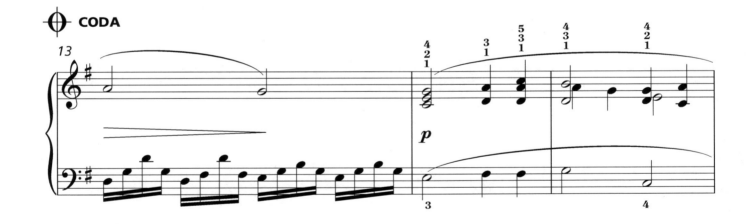

rit. e dim.

Old Music Box

Vitalij Neugasimov

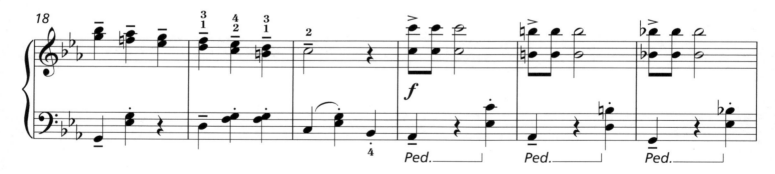

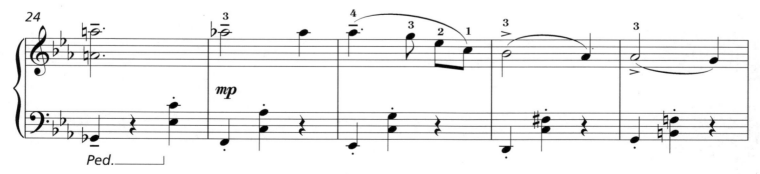

Space Wanderer

Vitalij Neugasimov

Dolce e misterioso ♩ = 96

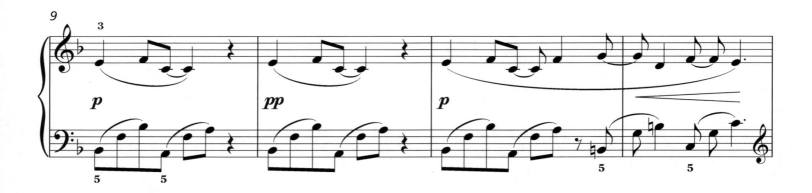

Poco meno mosso

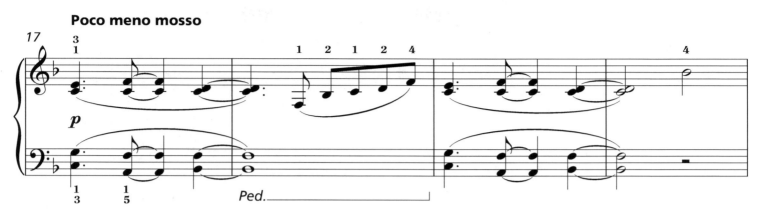

Tempo I

rit. e dim.

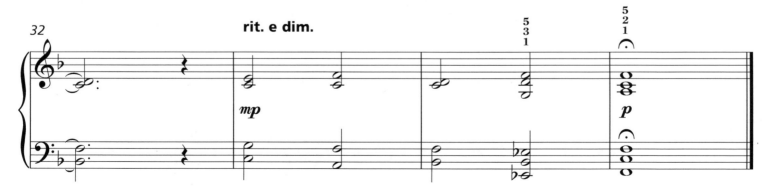

Menuet

Vitalij Neugasimov

Springtime

Vitalij Neugasimov

Con spirito ♩ = 144

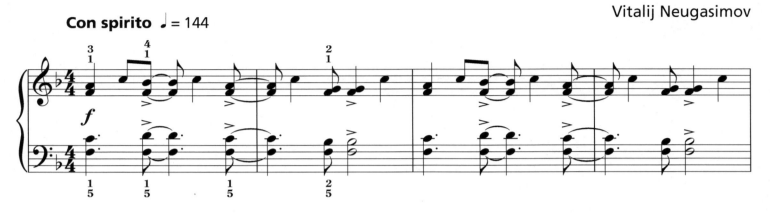

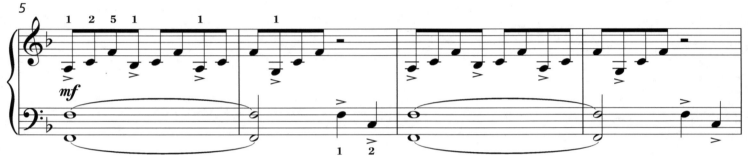

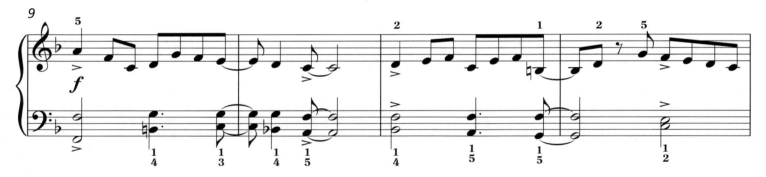

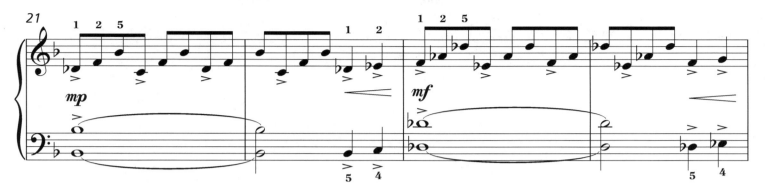

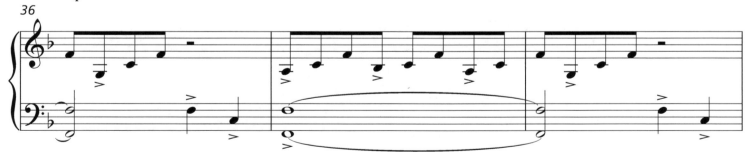

Your Eyes

Vitalij Neugasimov

Adagio con moto ♩ = 84

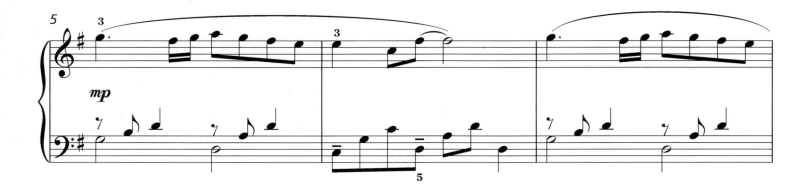

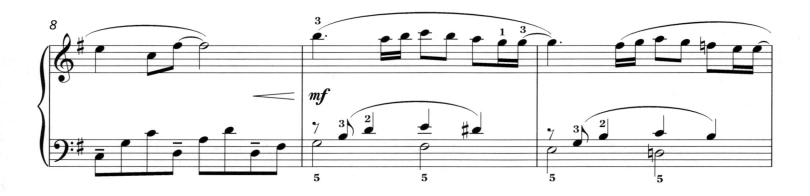

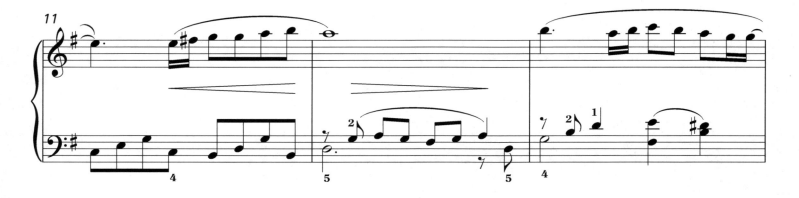

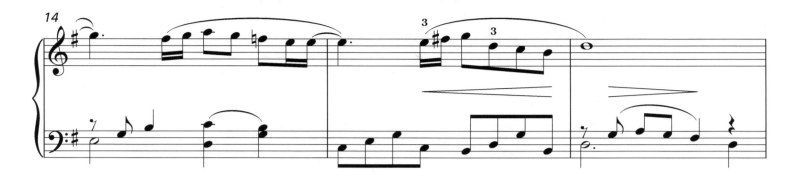

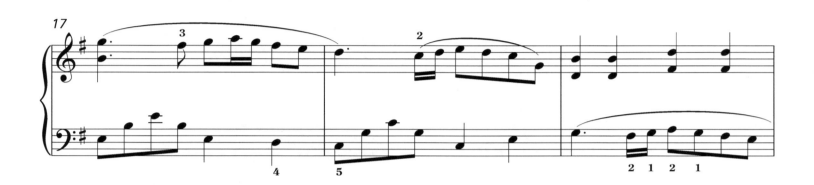

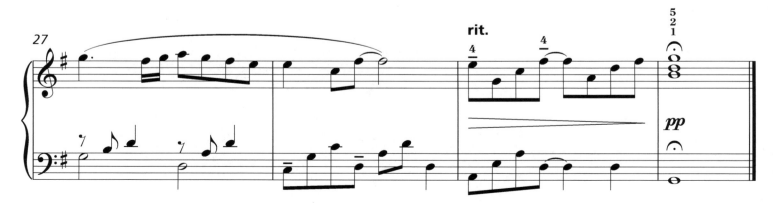

Once Upon a Time

Vitalij Neugasimov

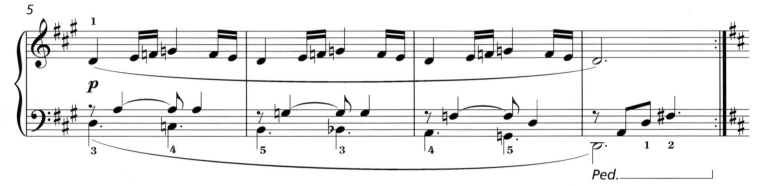

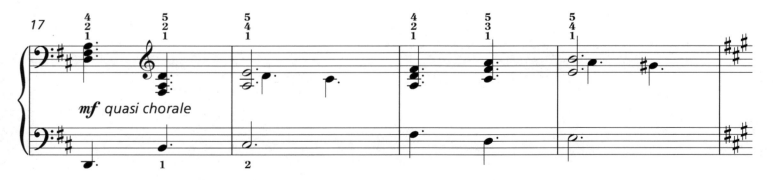

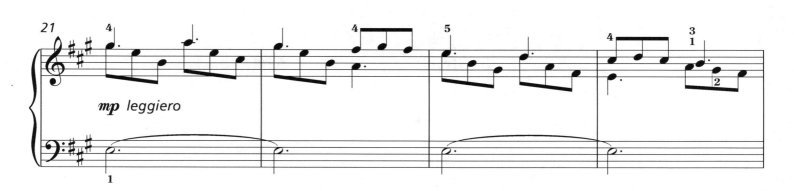

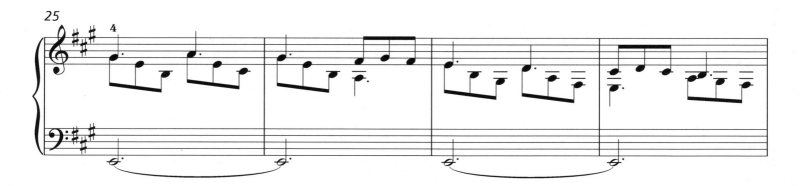

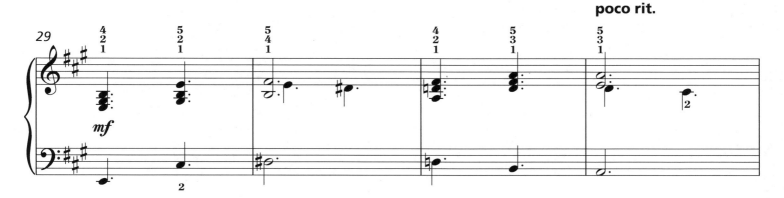

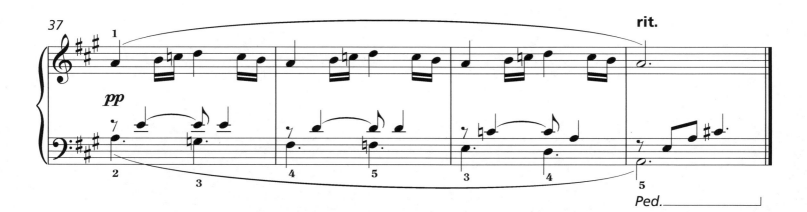

From Heart to Heart

Vitalij Neugasimov

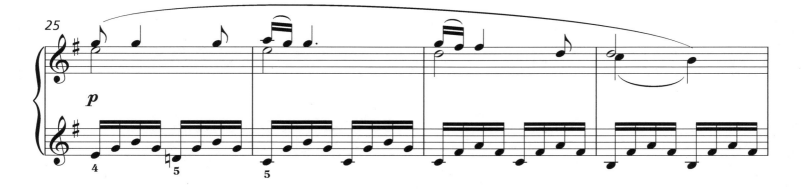

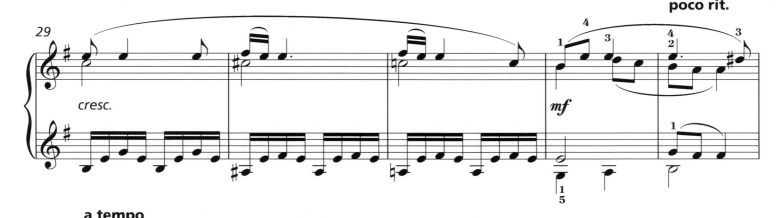

Sonatina Polifonica

Vitalij Neugasimov

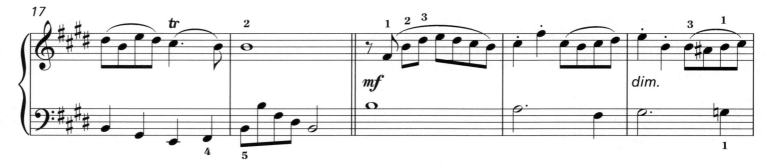

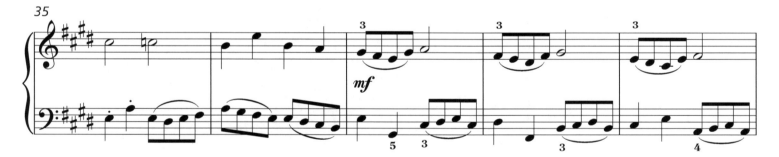

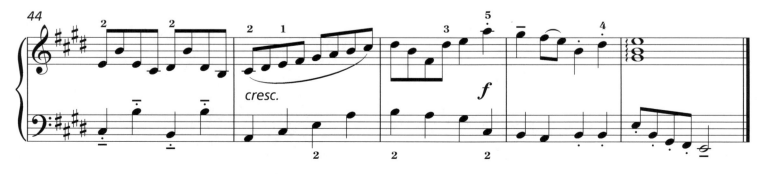